Visit the sick:

Ministering God's grace in times of illness

Brian Croft

DayOne

©Day One Publications 2008
Reprinted 2010

A CIP record is held at the British Library

ISBN 978-1-84625-143-6

Published by Day One Publications, Ryelands Road, Leominster, HR6 8NZ
☎ 01568 613 740
FAX 01568 611 473
email—sales@dayone.co.uk
web site—www.dayone.co.uk
North American e-mail—usasales@dayone.co.uk

Cover designed by Wayne McMaster and printed in the USA

To my father,
who taught me the value of this work through many
visits and house calls to his patients. Thank you for
graciously allowing me to accompany you.

In loving memory of
Ferrill Gardner,
known by those who knew him best as
'the master of the hospital room'.

COMMENDATIONS

What do pastors do when visiting the sick? Such visits are crucial both eternally and pastorally. Brian Croft has written a marvellous piece to assist us. His work is theologically grounded, gospel centred and full of practical wisdom. I recommend it enthusiastically.

> **Thomas R. Schreiner, James Buchanan Harrison Professor of New Testament Interpretation, The Southern Baptist Theological Seminary, and Teaching Pastor, Clifton Baptist Church**

I read Brian Croft's Visit the Sick *with glad thanksgiving! Visitation is a timely and much-needed topic for pastors and Christians in our day. And Croft addresses it with sound thinking and very helpful suggestions.* Visit the Sick *sets out to provide sensitive, God-honouring and gospel-driven counsel to pastors and Christians. And it hits the mark. If you're like me, someone who feels ill-equipped to say the right words or do the right things at someone's sickbed, you'll delight in this book and give God great praise for moving Brian Croft to write it. May the Lord be pleased to move us to visit our people and by that means awaken legions!*

> **Thabiti Anyabwile, Senior Pastor, First Baptist Church, Grand Cayman Island, and author,** The Faithful Preacher

Every pastor—and many other church leaders as well—will visit the sick. Some feel that their visits are fruitful times of ministry; others feel very awkward. Very, very few, however, have the intuitive people skills and the pastoral expertise to do this successfully without some training. Brian Croft's book provides concise, wise and practical instruction for this important aspect of ministry. Read it for yourself, study it as a staff or use it as a training resource for all those in your church who regularly visit the sick. It can help turn a routine responsibility into a time of effective ministry.

Donald Whitney, Associate Professor of Biblical Spirituality, The Southern Baptist Theological Seminary; President, The Center of Biblical Spirituality; and author, Spiritual Disciplines of the Christian Life

Visit the Sick *is an excellent and much-needed resource today when the actual practice of 'shepherding souls' is so often neglected. Many younger pastors (and not so young ones as well) have never received the sort of very practical guidance which Brian Croft gives in this book. This book has the potential to be a great blessing to pastors and those they shepherd. It will now be a recommended text in my Pastoral Ministries class and I heartily commend it to others.*

Ray Van Neste, Ph.D., Associate Professor of Christian Studies; Director, R. C. Ryan Center for Biblical Studies, Union University; and elder, Cornerstone Community Church

One of the primary reasons why so many Christians fail to heed Jesus' instruction to visit the sick is that they feel ill-prepared. What should I say? How long should I stay? Why should I go? What should I pray? What if the person is dying? What if he or she is not a Christian? Those are just a few of the many apprehensions people have about visiting the sick. In this very readable book, Brian Croft provides us with practical assistance that should eliminate feelings of inadequacy and motivate the reader to fulfil Christ's commission, 'I was sick and you visited me.' A biblically based, highly practical manual for Christian care-givers, this insightful book can be read in just a few minutes but its down-to-earth counsel will equip you to confidently visit the sick for years to come.

Bob Russell, former Senior Pastor, Southeast Christian Church, Louisville, Kentucky

One of the most vital aspects of pastoral ministry is seizing teachable moments in which the gospel of Christ can have its maximum impact. Times of suffering from sickness have the power to prepare the heart for the seed of the Word as few other things can. Brian Croft has done an excellent job of showing how the pastor can make the Word of God central in his ministry to the sick and dying. He does so with specific and practical counsel, and with words saturated with Scripture. I heartily commend this work as a benefit to the fruitful ministry of the gospel.

Dr Andrew Davis, Senior Pastor, First Baptist Church, Durham, North Carolina, and author, An Approach To Extended Memorization of Scripture

Brian Croft has served us all well in providing a succinct, thoughtful training manual for hospital visitation. Church member, let this book equip you to become more useful to those in your church who are ailing. Young pastor, gain from Brian's practical wisdom. Let him train you to love and serve your congregation in a way that will adorn your preaching (and help you avoid awkward mistakes). Seasoned pastor, let this book remind you of the privilege it is to serve and encourage the sick in a fallen world. I plan to read it together with my elders, and hope to make it available to my congregation as an equipping tool.

Paul Alexander, Senior Pastor, Fox Valley Bible Church, St Charles, Illinois, and co-author, The Deliberate Church

Brian has given us a practical and theological guide to caring for our congregations. It is a must-read for those interested in a theology for visiting the sick.

Dr George D. Barnett, Ministry Resource Consultant, Georgia Baptist Convention

Seldom does one encounter pastoral resources of a practical nature that are richly biblical and theologically grounded. But Brian Croft's excellent guide to pastoral visitation of the sick and ailing is exactly that. By placing his wise and perceptive practical counsel within the framework of key biblical teaching and central theological conviction, he provides more than a mere 'how to' guide for pastoral visitation. Thankfully, he also offers the gospel of grace and power needed for the kind of practical help that truly brings honour to God and leads people to Christ. Filled with wisdom and rooted in theology, this resource offers the blend so needed in the church today.

Bruce A. Ware, Professor of Christian Theology, The Southern Baptist Theological Seminary, and author, God's Lesser Glory: The Diminished God of Open Theism

ACKNOWLEDGEMENTS

A special thanks to:

The many faithful labourers who read over this manuscript and gave their helpful input. Your comments and counsel were of immense value. I want especially to thank the tireless labour of my fellow labourers in the gospel: Scott, Adam, Greg and Matt, whose time and gifts towards this project I could never repay.

Day One Publications, for seeing the value in this work, and especially Jim Holmes, for your excitement and encouragement through the process.

Heather Peterson, for sharing your amazing gift of editing by serving me on this project. It has been a joy to work with you.

The faithful saints of Auburndale Baptist Church, for allowing me the gift of your fellowship, the encouragement of your love, and your endless support of my labour in the Word for the sake of your souls. I gain great joy from watching God further the gospel and build his church through your desire for, submission to and worship of him.

Mark Dever, not only for writing the Foreword, but also for the many years of invaluable investment, teaching, instruction and guidance you have given me.

Don Whitney, for your wisdom, counsel and guidance throughout the writing of this book. Learning from you in this way has been a precious gift.

My father, for your endless encouragement in this project, as well as for your powerful and selfless example to me my whole life of what it means to care not just for the physical but also for the spiritual needs of others.

My children: Samuel, Abby, Isabelle and Claire. What unspeakable joy you bring me by your love, care and affection! You remain a daily example to me of God's undeserved goodness and grace.

My wife: you remain the most compelling example of this book by your unconditional care of me. Apart from my Saviour, there is no one I love more than you.

Our sovereign, eternal God and King Jesus, who pardons all our iniquities, heals all our diseases (Ps. 103:3), and in his infinite wisdom and mystery displays himself most powerfully in our weakness (2 Cor. 12:9).

CONTENTS

FOREWORD

I remember the first time when I did hospital visitation. I was twenty-one or twenty-two. I had just begun to work in a church, and the senior pastor asked me to go and visit some older members in the hospital. And let me make it clear: these were 'older members' who had been born in the previous century! I didn't know any of them. They certainly wouldn't know me. What would I have to give them? What could I contribute to them? The deep and self-conscious awkwardness of feeling useless came over me.

God was very kind to me on that first day of visitation. And over the weeks and months to come, I made many more visits to that hospital and others on the north shore of Boston. Oh, how I wish that this little book had existed then! What frustration and embarrassment it might have saved me! How it would have served those I was trying to encourage!

Brian Croft is well qualified to help the pastor in this way. He himself is a faithful pastor, accustomed to visiting the sick in hospital. I've known Brian for a number of years. His father, Bill Croft, is a physician and a wonderful Christian man. So Brian has grown up among those concerned for the sick. His brother, Scott Croft, has served on staff with me at the Capitol Hill Baptist Church in Washington and is currently serving as the chairman of our elders. Scott has been an encouragement to, instructor to and student of Brian. Brian's sister, Beth Spraul, is a member of my congregation and has served in hospital chaplaincies. So, from many angles, Brian is a man well qualified to advise us in these matters.

In this little volume, Brian helps us to think straightforwardly and faithfully about God's truth and God's people. His advice is as sound as it is simple. Some parts of this book may be about matters you've already worked out. But isn't it better to be told something twice than not at all? Let Brian's be that reinforcing voice. And don't be surprised if you read some things that you hadn't thought of before. Read this book, and let Brian help you help others.

Mark Dever

Senior Pastor, Capitol Hill Baptist Church, Washington, DC

PREFACE

We are victims of our own culture. The twenty-first century has brought with it demands, pressures and deadlines that have left us feeling as if our lives are often spinning out of control. We have all felt the tension of trying to balance time with God, work, family, church, school, social occasions, house repairs, personal errands and sleep, all of which need our daily attention. Unfortunately, we often come to the end of the day exhausted, wondering where the time went. Our day becomes reminiscent of the hamster running in his wheel—busy, but going nowhere. It is this tension that leads to the neglect of certain essential responsibilities in the life of a Christian. One of those essential tasks is the visiting and care of the sick within our churches.

My goal with this book is to instruct and motivate us to recapture this God-honouring practice and to do so by reaching for a standard that, frankly, is beyond us today. This means that we must be taught by those who lived at a different time within a different culture. We must learn from those who modelled an astounding dedication to this call. We must learn from their accounts and convictions. We must be instructed by our heroes from church history.

Perhaps the greatest historical example of visiting the afflicted was the seventeenth-century Puritan pastor Richard Baxter. Baxter had an amazing strategy of visiting not just the sick but everyone in his congregation throughout Kidderminster regularly and faithfully. In the midst of his much-disciplined routine, Baxter developed a certain sensitivity to those in his congregation who were sick and homebound. He wrote in *The Reformed Pastor*, 'We must be diligent in visiting the sick, and helping them to prepare either for a fruitful life, or a happy death.'[1]

Many others in Baxter's time and since were found to be diligent in this task, yet as society made its turn into the twentieth century, the local church and its priorities began to change. Somewhere in the midst of industrialized nations and changing churches, the care for the sick began gradually to diminish. It is for this reason that we must go back beyond the twentieth century to seek a historical model if we are to recapture caring for the sick in a way that most glorifies God in our modern day.

There are, however, a few challenges to this approach. It would be difficult on several levels for a pastor today to achieve the standard of care that Baxter and other Puritans maintained. My solution is to take their principles and try to paint a picture of what they would realistically look like today. We must also recognize that Baxter, Spurgeon and other Puritan-like pastors would have absolutely no category to relate to the hyper-sensitive, self-consumed mindset we find rampant in our twenty-first-century culture. Some adjustments are therefore necessary, especially in regard to the practicality of visiting hospitals, nursing homes, rehabilitation centres and the homes of those who are saturated in our secular environment today.

The application found in this book is the result of my humble attempt to balance the example of these heroes of church history with those necessary adjustments. I pray that your labour in reading this (and mine in writing) will not be in vain. May we have an awakening towards the care and fellowship of those often forgotten in our congregations. Ultimately, may this work lead to a rediscovery of what the Bible portrays as a true Christian community embodying a visual picture of the gospel.

I owe a significant debt to the faithful elderly saints of Auburndale Baptist Church. Thank you so much for your example of faith and unshakable hope in the gospel throughout your numerous sicknesses and sufferings. No one has taught me more about the sufficiency of our Saviour than so many of you. Thank you, not only for the gift of allowing me to care for you through your sicknesses, but also for your clear and powerful portrayal of Christ in the midst of them by your joy.

Brian Croft

Auburndale Baptist Church, Louisville, Kentucky

INTRODUCTION

Before considering the practical aspects of visiting the sick, you may need to be more convinced that this task is important not only for pastors but also for all members of the local church. Let us therefore take a moment to consider the reasons why this should be a priority in our lives as Christians and is worthy of our attention.

First of all, visiting the sick is biblical. The apostle James exhorts those who are sick to call for the elders of the church to pray over them (James 5:14). Christians are also encouraged to pray in a like manner (James 5:16). It was Jesus who taught the care for the sick as a primary way to love him and our brother (Matt. 25:36, 40) and who led by example (Mark 1:31). The apostles followed this pattern of caring for the sick (Acts 3:7; 28:8). The widows were especially to be cared for (1 Tim. 5:3–10). Caring for the sick is part of caring for souls, something for which leaders will give an account (Heb. 13:17). In my quick referencing of these passages, it needs to be acknowledged that they have a specific purpose and meaning within the context of their writing. However, we can still glean helpful principles from them to apply to this task. Jesus and the apostles cared about the sick and afflicted. They exhorted others to do so too.

Visiting the sick also gives a tremendous opportunity to minister to and to love our fellow Christians. Charles Spurgeon wisely stated, 'I venture to say that the greatest earthly blessing that God can give to any of us is health, with the exception of sickness. Sickness has frequently been of more use to the saints of God than health has.'[2] There is a spiritual attentiveness that accompanies sickness that easily fizzles in health. As we look for ways to care for one another as Christians, may we seize those moments that God in his kindness provides.

We must also be convinced that this is the calling not only of pastors and leaders in the church, but of all in the church:

pastors, deacons and teachers; singles and married people; men and women; and families as well. We must see this as similar to the early church's dedication to provide for the needs of the church (Acts 2 and 4): as the calling and responsibility of all covenant members of a local church to one another. It is important that we do not underestimate the impact that visiting those who are sick and afflicted can have on each of us. The nineteenth-century Scottish pastor David Dickson wrote, 'On the bed of sickness the Lord ripens his people for glory, and to the elder himself it is often a scene of instruction and revival.'[3] God will not only sanctify the sick through sickness, but he will also teach and encourage the healthy through the same means. May each of us therefore mature in our love for God and for one another and see the benefit, as well as the call, upon each of our lives to care for the sick. Let us begin by considering the biblical evidence on this matter.

Biblical considerations

I was sick, and you visited Me.

–Matt. 25:36

The lens through which we view life as Christians is the Bible, because it is the foundation of all we are and know about God. Misunderstandings about God and his purposes are directly linked to a failure to know the full storyline of the Bible. We must, therefore, read and understand the Bible in its full context of redemptive history if we are to interpret correctly its truth for the individual issues of our lives.

The aim of this chapter is to demonstrate God's purposes and ways as they unfold in the storyline of the Bible in relation to sickness, disease and suffering. The reality of sickness and disease is found throughout Scripture. However, we need to know not just the verses in the Bible on sickness, disease and suffering, but also how God is working his purpose in them for the good of his people and his glory. This is most clearly seen in considering the progression of Scripture from Genesis to Revelation on this issue. The unfolding storyline also reveals the undeniable presence of two themes: that God is sovereign over sickness and healing, and that God calls his people to care for the needy and afflicted.

Creation

The Bible begins its historical narrative with a world that is foreign to us today. God created the heavens, the earth and all the living creatures (Gen. 1–2). He also created man and woman in his image (1:27) and saw that all that he had made was very good (1:31). He placed the man and woman in the Garden of Eden, where they were to rule over his creation and be fruitful and multiply. The garden was beautiful, and in it there flowed a river to water the garden and a tree of life that was good for food (2:9–10). This was a world that was perfectly made: man was created in the image of God, man enjoyed unhindered fellowship with God, and man ruled over the creation while fully submitting to God's rule over him.

In this world, there was also an absence of sickness, pain, disease, suffering and affliction. No cancer preyed upon the human body. No aches and pains plagued the body. No disease needed to be healed, nor did any sickness at all need to be cured. Most significantly, there was no death. All was good, perfect and right, as God intended for his creation.

Fall

Nevertheless, this world in Genesis 1–2 is not the world we live in today. The reality now is that there is something really wrong with the world and with those who were made in God's image. This more familiar understanding of the world is traced back to Genesis 3, where Adam and Eve sinned by disobeying God's word and eating of the tree of the knowledge of good and evil (3:6). God told Adam and Eve not to eat from this tree or they would die (2:17). Satan tempted Eve, and she ate from the tree and gave some of its fruit to her husband (3:6). Instead of obeying God's command, they rebelled against him. They wanted to rule, not to be ruled by God.

As a result of their sin, the curse of death of which God had warned them came upon them and all his creation. On that day, sin with all its ramifications entered the world. Adam and Eve were removed from the garden and the tree of life, whose fruit would grant eternal life (3:22). There was now to be pain in childbirth (3:16). Man's task of working and ruling over the creation became hard and painful. A great separation from their once-unhindered fellowship with God now existed. Most significantly, death entered the world with sin and affected all creation, including man created in the image of God. As a result, man would suffer not only death, but also all the effects of death, such as old age, pain and suffering.

Sickness and disease are therefore here revealed as part of the curse. There are many explanations today about what sickness really is and how it came to exist. The Bible, however, simplifies a complicated topic. Sickness, disease, pain, suffering, affliction and death are undeniable evidences of the fall of man. From this point in the storyline of the Bible, the desperate need for redemption begins. It is quickly revealed in the narrative that only a sovereign, eternal God can intervene to save creation from this curse. The hope of the gospel, which includes the promise of physical resurrection, therefore now begins to unfold in a glorious work of redemption that culminates in Jesus' death and resurrection.

The life of Israel

God decided to redeem mankind through a chosen nation that would be his people among all the other nations of the earth. This nation was promised to Abraham (Gen. 12) through a child, Isaac, who would be born (Gen. 21). From this child, the nation of Israel (Jacob, the son of Isaac) would begin. Through Isaac's grandson, Joseph, the nation of Israel was established in Egypt, where they multiplied greatly (Exod. 1:7), yet the people eventually became enslaved to the Egyptians. God, however, had promised hundreds of years before this (Gen. 15:13–14) that he would deliver them from their oppression and judge the nation which held them captive. Through the events of this deliverance, God would use sickness and disease for his purposes and glory.

Moses went to Pharaoh and requested that he free God's people from their enslavement. Pharaoh refused, which led to a series of judgements that fell upon the Egyptians. A number of the judgements were related to diseases on the livestock and painful sores upon the people (Exod. 9). The final judgement that fell upon Pharaoh was the death of all the firstborn children (Exod. 12). In his sovereign power, God both inflicted disease as judgement upon the Egyptians and protected his people,

Israel. God's use of disease as judgement upon sin explains why God said, 'If you will give earnest heed to the voice of the LORD your God, and do what is right in His sight, and give ear to His commandments, and keep all His statutes, I will put none of the diseases on you which I have put on the Egyptians; for I, the LORD, am your healer' (Exod. 15:26). God had displayed his faithfulness to Israel and his power to protect them.

Tragically, the Bible reveals from Israel's history in the wilderness that they did not obey the covenant which God made with them (Exod. 19). In this Old Covenant, God promised blessing for obedience and curses for disobedience. A significant number of the curses that resulted from disobedience to God's law were related to sickness and disease. Ceremonial uncleanness to the law was identified by certain diseases such as leprosy, infection and other sicknesses (Lev. 13–14). Moses listed these specifics related to sickness in Deuteronomy 28: pestilence, consumption, fever, boils, tumours, scabs, madness, blindness, famine, hunger, thirst, miserable and chronic sicknesses, and plagues. All these pointed to God's curse upon his people for not obeying all his commandments and statutes (Deut. 28:15). These examples reveal God's use of sickness and disease as judgement, but also his sovereign power to heal.

God showed his mercy in healing Miriam from leprosy because Moses asked God to heal her (Num. 12:9–15). In this example, we also find the presence of compassion and care for the afflicted. Aaron pleaded with Moses to ask God for mercy on her behalf. Her healing came about because of the burden Aaron felt towards her affliction, which led to Moses' asking God to heal her. God not only honoured the request of Aaron, but he also showed his compassionate heart towards Miriam in affliction.

The evidence of God's purposes in sickness and disease continued in both judgement and healing as Israel entered the promised land and established human kings to rule over them.

God caused King David's son to become sick and die because of David's adultery (2 Sam. 12:14–18). King Asa became diseased in his feet. Though his disease was severe, he sought physicians instead of the Lord and died (2 Chr. 16:12–13). Yet God's powerful hand brought healing to King Hezekiah, who was mortally ill and had been told that he would die (2 Kings 20:1–11). God brought healing to a little boy through Elijah as a result of the mother's plea to the Lord (1 Kings 17:17–24). In the midst of judgement upon disobedience, God also showed his kindness.

The picture of relief and hope from the curses of God upon sin developed strongly in Israel's history through the time of the prophets and Israel's exile. The prophets brought hope of redemption through the figurative use of sickness/healing. The prophet Jeremiah spoke of the heart that was 'desperately sick' (Jer. 17:9), yet it was the Lord who was his people's hope (17:13) and who would heal and save (17:14). The prophet Isaiah inspired hope in the Redeemer, the Messiah, who was to be pierced for our transgressions, crushed for our iniquities and scourged for our healing (Isa. 53:5). With the prophets, the healing of sickness ultimately described God's saving work and forgiveness of sins. This is evidenced in the words of the psalmist, who hoped in the God who pardons all our iniquities and heals all our diseases (Ps. 103:3). The prophets pointed to redemption by means of a spiritual healing by a sovereign God, who would heal and save from spiritual sickness through the Messiah to come.

God's unfolding storyline of redemption also reveals the call upon his people to care for those who suffer the affliction of sickness and disease. God, through the prophet Ezekiel, chastised the shepherds of Israel for neglecting their flock. They neglected the people of God in several ways, but one in particular was in not caring for the sick. Ezekiel wrote, 'Those who are sickly you have not strengthened, the diseased you have not healed, the broken you have not bound up, the scattered you have not brought back, nor have you sought for the lost; but with force and with severity you have dominated them' (Ezek. 34:4). The shepherds' neglecting to care for the sick would naturally lead to the people's neglect in the same way.

Throughout Israel's history, God used sickness, disease and affliction as part of a divine design to achieve his purposes. The prophets concluded that God's people were scattered, disobedient and discouraged, yet encouraged them to wait for the hope of the promised Redeemer and Healer. Despite this tragic history of God's people, God was faithful to the covenant he made with his people to send a Redeemer and usher in the long-awaited kingdom of God.

The life of Christ

After many years of silence, God broke through the despair and suffering with a voice of one crying out in the wilderness to make ready the way of the Lord (Mark 1:3). This voice was John the Baptist, who was the forerunner to come and prepare others for the coming of the Redeemer. All four Gospels identify Jesus as this Redeemer, the long-awaited Messiah who was to save his people from their sins and usher in the kingdom of God. Mark points us to Jesus Christ the Redeemer in Jesus' first recorded words in his Gospel account: 'The time is fulfilled, and the kingdom of God is at hand; repent and believe in the gospel' (Mark 1:15). The kingdom was brought near by Jesus.

Throughout his account, Mark displayed the evidence that Jesus came with the authority of God as the Son of God (Mark 1:1); a primary evidence of the coming of this kingdom in him was his authority over sickness, disease and death. All the Gospel writers remind the reader of this reality in similar summaries: 'The news about Him spread throughout all Syria; and they brought to Him all who were ill, those suffering with various diseases and pains, demoniacs, epileptics, paralytics;

and He healed them' (Matt. 4:24). Jesus healed many and thus fulfilled the prophets' words.

John also demonstrated this fulfilment of the prophets. John wrote of a man blind from birth who encountered Jesus (John 9:1–7). In verse 2, the disciples ask a question that would be very common in light of Israel's natural experience of sickness and judgement: 'Rabbi, who sinned, this man or his parents, that he would be born blind?' The transition from Israel's bondage to the coming kingdom is seen in Jesus' response: 'It was neither that this man sinned, nor his parents; but it was so that the works of God might be displayed in him' (v. 3). John points us not just to the healing, but also to the display of God's work of redemption through the work of his Son.

This evidence of Jesus' authority and the coming kingdom is most clearly seen in Jesus' raising of the dead. Jesus revived the synagogue official's little girl who had died (Mark 5:41–42). He raised Lazarus from the dead after days of his being in the tomb (John 11:44). Ultimately, Jesus' raising of the dead pointed to his own physical resurrection from the dead three days after dying on the cross. In the Messiah's own resurrection, his followers are promised not only eternal life through repentance and faith in him, but also a physical resurrection on the final day: 'For if we have become united with Him in the likeness of His death, certainly we shall also be in the likeness of His resurrection' (Rom. 6:5). In this resurrection, his followers have the promise of being children of the eternal kingdom of God.

God's sovereign power over sickness and disease in Jesus' authority is undeniable throughout the Gospel accounts, but we must not miss the call Jesus gave to his followers to care for those who were afflicted. The clearest example of this is in Matthew 25, where Jesus teaches his disciples a parable about kingdom living in caring for others in his name: 'For I was hungry, and you gave Me something to eat; I was thirsty, and you gave Me something to drink; I was a stranger, and you invited Me in;

naked and you clothed Me; I was sick, and you visited Me; I was in prison, and you came to Me' (Matt. 25:35–36). Jesus continued, powerfully teaching that they cared for their King in those moments when they cared for the least of their brothers (v. 40). He ended this teaching by speaking of the judgement that would fall on the wicked who showed that they did not care for him by their neglect to care for others (vv. 41–46).

Jesus ushered in the kingdom of God, and a primary evidence that redemption has come is that the blind see, the lame walk, the deaf hear, the sick and diseased are healed, and the dead are raised. God has designed his people to care for one another as a powerful representation of his compassion for the weak and needy. As the narrative continues to unfold, these glorious evidences of the kingdom of God are further seen in the birth and life of Christ's church.

The life of the church

When Jesus sent out his disciples, he commanded them to 'Heal the sick, raise the dead, cleanse the lepers, cast out demons' (Matt. 10:8). These commands came to fulfilment as the church was birthed at Pentecost (Acts 2) and as the apostles went out as Christ's witnesses to the world (Acts 1:8). Through the apostles, we find God's sovereign power to judge, as well as heal, according to his purposes. Ananias and Sapphira received divine judgement in death because they lied about giving the full portion of the proceeds from their sold property to the apostles (5:1–11). God also used healing as a measure of compassion upon Tabitha and those who loved her; after she fell sick and died, Peter raised her from the dead (9:36–43).

God's sovereign redemptive purposes in sickness and suffering are also seen in the letters of the apostles. Paul was given a thorn in his flesh so that the power of Christ would be most powerfully displayed in his weakness (2 Cor. 12:8–9). Sickness and death were used as means to warn the church against abusing the

Lord's Table (1 Cor. 11:30). Peter urged Christians who suffered according to the will of God to see this as a time to entrust their souls to their faithful Creator (1 Peter 4:19). The sovereign God of the universe has used sickness, pain, disease and suffering as a way to sanctify his kingdom people and magnify the worth of Christ.

There is also a call for those in the church to care sacrificially for the afflicted in order to achieve these redemptive purposes. A powerful example of this calling comes in the book of Acts when Christians sell their properties and lay the proceeds at the apostles' feet to be used to serve those in need (4:34–37). Paul referred to Epaphroditus' sickness when he wrote to the church in Philippi, and care and concern from both Paul and the church are evident in this matter (Phil. 2:25–27). James exhorted Christians to call upon the elders to pray for the sick (James 5:14). John prayed for the Christians 'that in all respects you may prosper and be in good health, just as your soul prospers' (3 John 1:2). In these examples, there is sympathy for the sick and needy. The call of sacrificial action to one another exists for the Christian. There remains a trust in God's sovereign design to be accomplished in sickness, but the individual Christian and the local church body are called to care for those within the church who are sick, hurting, afflicted and suffering, until Jesus returns for his church and consummates his kingdom.

New creation
The unfolding of God's redemptive plan for all creation will reach a conclusion. The final destination for those who follow Christ is not a disembodied existence of life after death. When Jesus returns, he will come for his bride, judge the nations, punish the wicked and fully consummate his kingdom in the new heaven and new earth. This state is known as the new creation, where the curse of sin is fully and permanently reversed. There God's

kingdom people will experience not just physical resurrection, but also eternal fellowship with Jesus their Saviour and King.

A wonderful hope for us in this coming promise is that we will have physically whole bodies that are not cursed. In other words, there will be no more sickness, disease, pain, suffering, affliction and death. John gives us a very vivid picture of this in the book of Revelation as he writes, 'He will wipe away every tear from their eyes; and there will no longer be any death; there will no longer be any mourning, or crying, or pain' (Rev. 21:4). Reminding us of Eden (Gen. 2), John also speaks of a centrally located river and tree of life whose leaves are for the healing of the nations (Rev. 22:1–2). The curse has been reversed and those who belong to the kingdom of God through the cross of Christ will experience what God intended in the Garden of Eden.

Understanding this unfolding storyline of the Bible is essential not only for grasping God's design and plan for his creation, but also for comprehending God's eternal purpose in the reality of sickness, disease, pain and affliction in the world. In the midst of the sickness or affliction that someone in our church may be experiencing, we have the glorious privilege of pointing to a greater, divine and more significant reality than that person's physical circumstances. We can point to sickness and affliction as results of the Fall and to our dying bodies as reminders of our birth in sin. We can remind others that sickness was a means for God to discipline his chosen people that caused them to long for a Redeemer. We can rejoice that the signs of God's kingdom coming were the healings and restorations by the authority of the Son of God—a foretaste of what we will experience in full when Jesus returns and resurrection becomes a reality.

The Bible's teaching on sickness and disease should also move us to respond in worship to our great, eternal and sovereign God who controls sickness and healing in his infinite wisdom for the good of his people and his own glory. We should also respond with a great burden to care for those who are sick, afflicted and needy, because of the biblical responsibility that is clearly before all of us who follow Christ. May these considerations of biblical truth prepare us not only for our own afflictions that are certain to come, but also to care sacrificially for those in our churches who long to experience the fellowship of Jesus through our faithful care of them in their afflictions. In so doing, we fulfil the words of Christ: '"When did we see You sick, or in prison, and come to You?" The King will answer and say to them, "Truly I say to you, to the extent that you did it to one of these brothers of Mine, even the least of them, you did it to Me"' (Matt. 25:39–40). May we be faithful to do likewise.

Within this biblical framework, let us now move to theological considerations.

Theological considerations

I venture to say that the greatest earthly blessing that God can give to any of us is health, with the exception of sickness.

–Charles Spurgeon

D octrine lays the foundation for application. The apostle Paul modelled this pattern in his letters of the New Testament. Many of the great Christian preachers in history have borrowed this approach. It is this same approach that will guide us to effective spiritual care of the sick. We may be effective practically and wise pastorally, but if our care is void of the hope of the gospel and the promises in God's Word, any hope or encouragement will be an illusion. We should therefore consider these theological suggestions for the benefit of the souls of those for whom we desire to care, as well as for our own good.

Ask leading questions

We must be deliberate about our conversations when visiting the sick. If we are going to be faithful in this task, we need to anticipate having to lead these interactions. The best way to prepare is to consider what kinds of questions we would like to ask that will eventually lead to spiritual conversation. As we prepare, however, we must remember to whom we are talking. Sick people are, at the very least, uncomfortable because of their circumstances. They may also be dealing with intense pain, be in and out of consciousness, or be distracted by other family members in the room. Before we begin to ask questions, therefore, we should heed the wise counsel of David Dickson: 'Don't let us strain them with anything requiring long or continuous attention, and let our change from one subject to another be natural and easy.'[4] Only after we have given thoughtful consideration to what we should ask should we then proceed. Here is a progression that has seemed to be helpful for myself and others. Ask the sick about themselves, their conditions, and what kinds of treatment are being carried out. Ask about their families, specifically with regard to those who have been caring for them during this time. Then, in some way, try to turn the conversations to those of a spiritual nature. A helpful way to do this is to ask how you can pray for them. Through this question, the Holy Spirit often opens opportunities for talking about eternal issues. How are they struggling? How are they relating to God through this? The most important theological question to ask, if appropriate, is, 'Are you ready to die and stand before God?'[5] We ask questions to learn about their situations and how they are handling them. This is essential in knowing how best to care for them and, most importantly, their souls. However, our questions are to lead us to talk about God and their hope only found in Christ. This is our aim, whether they are sick or healthy. Therefore, our questions should be sensitive to their circumstances, but God-honouring and gospel-driven in content.

Read Scripture

A young seminary student in my church decided to visit a dying member in hospital. He had very little experience, yet heard me challenge the congregation to care for this long-time, faithful member during this sudden turn for the worse. He walked into her hospital room to find the woman in a most disturbing state. She was semi-conscious, gasping for every breath and having seizures. He also stumbled in on a very unusual occurrence—no family in the room. He had heard me say, 'There is always family in the room to talk to.' This time, there was not. What would you have done? This faithful brother had an effective and spiritually mature response.

He opened his Bible and began to read. As he stood over the bed of this dying woman gasping for breath, he read about the glorious character of God and his faithful promises to his adopted children in Christ. The woman passed away soon after this faithful brother left the room. Only God knows the fruit of that afternoon. But we need to see how sound his instincts were in that moment. It is God's Word that is living and active and sharper than any two-edged sword (Heb. 4:12). We must have the truth of God's Word on our lips; otherwise, we may not respond well when faced with such an uncomfortable moment.

How can we prepare for these types of situations? Think through several Scriptures that might be an encouragement to the sick. It is helpful to think of these passages in categories. Here are four categories with examples that may be helpful in a variety of situations:

- Passages of comfort (Ps. 23; 28; 34; 46; 62; 145; Heb. 4:14–16)
- Succinct gospel passages (John 11:25–26; Rom. 5:6–11; Eph. 2:1–10; 2 Cor. 5:17–21)
- Passages dealing with the purpose of suffering for the believer (2 Cor. 12:7–9; James 1:2–4; 1 Peter 1:6–7; 4:12–19)
- Passages relating to the reality and hope of eternity with Christ (John 10:27–30; John 14:1–3; Phil. 1:21–23; 1 Peter 1:3–5).

Having a few passages in your mind will allow you to be better equipped for the unexpected. Just in case you missed the obvious, bring your Bible.

Pray the gospel

One morning, I was called by a nurse at a local hospital who requested my immediate presence. The non-Christian spouse of one of our members was moments away from dying. I had no idea what awaited me when I arrived. I walked into a room full of family members, with the heartbroken husband motioning me over to his wife's bed. He himself was also suffering from some medical problems that resulted in a tracheotomy, preventing him from speaking. It did not take me long to see why I had been summoned. The husband was asking me to pray over his wife as the doctor removed the ventilator. Twenty minutes earlier, I had been in my office, neck-deep in my studies. Now, I found myself being asked to pray a final prayer over a dying non-Christian woman in front of her husband and fifteen to twenty non-Christian family members, who were hanging on to some miracle with my prayer. I had literally just a few seconds to decide what to do and how to pray.

I decided to pray the gospel for this dying woman, her husband and this room full of non-Christian family members. I did not pray for God to spare her. I did not pray that God would heal her. I did not pray some manipulating request that God would receive her (which is what I think they expected me to pray). Rather I prayed that the gospel was her only hope in such a way that God could let all the people in that room know that it was their only hope also. Praying the gospel does not have to be complicated. It could be something as simple as:

> Father in heaven, as we are reminded at this moment of the fragility of life and the reality of our own mortality, we thank you that you remain righteous, just and holy in all your ways as God and our Creator. We confess that we have rebelled against your perfect Word and character, and deserve your just wrath and punishment because of our sins. Yet we thank you that you are rich in mercy and have provided a way for us to escape this judgement and be eternally reconciled to you. This hope is found only through your own Son having died on the cross in our place and having been raised from the dead to give us new life. How great is your love that you would allow your perfect Son to die in the place of sinners, absorbing and satisfying your wrath so that we

could be made righteous before you! O God, thank you that this gracious offer of salvation comes, not by our own works, but by turning from our sins and trusting, by faith, in the person and work of Jesus. Father, may this be the hope and joy of us all, whether healthy or moments from death, so that you and your gospel would be known and glorified.

In the hospital room that day, God taught me an invaluable lesson that has had a profound impact on me and my ministry. When the gospel is prayed, the gospel is heard. When I prayed the gospel in that room, it was in the hearing of this dying woman moments from facing judgement, her Christian husband and her lost family members. If we truly believe that faith comes by hearing (Rom. 10:17), we should never leave a hospital room or ward, nursing home, rehabilitation centre or home of a sick person (or healthy person, for that matter) without praying the hope of God in Christ.

In the midst of attempting spiritual conversation when you visit, the ideal is to speak about God's righteousness, man's sinfulness and Christ's dying on the cross in our place for our sins. Many circumstances can, however, make that difficult. But nothing prevents us from praying the gospel. It is God alone through his Holy Spirit who transforms the darkest heart. We should see every visit as a divine appointment to make the saving power of the gospel known, whether through prayer or proclamation.

Affirm the promises and attributes of God

It is God's promises through his Word that expose all other false hopes. However, it is not just the promises of God alone that give us hope, but also the fact that we know and trust the God who gave these promises. Before affirming the promises, point the afflicted to the God of these promises. Use Scripture to bring to life the truth that the Lord is 'righteous in all His ways and kind in all His deeds' (Ps. 145:17). Remind them that God is sovereign over all things, including their afflictions. Encourage them to know that God is omniscient (knows all things), omnipotent (all-powerful), omnipresent (everywhere), faithful, loving and perfectly just, even as they suffer.

Once you have lifted up the faithful, unchanging character of God, read to them the promises of God for his chosen people in Christ. Read to them the promise that nothing can separate them from the love of God that is in Christ Jesus (Rom. 8:39). Remind them that God is their refuge and strength in distress (Ps. 59:16). Encourage them that their soul's hope is in God alone (Ps. 42:11). It is essential that, when we leave, we can have peace that we left more of God's character and promises than our own wisdom and thoughts on their minds and hearts.

Trust God's sovereign plan

We must be deliberate with our efforts. We must continually examine our hearts through these matters for our own sanctification and growth. But, ultimately, it is a sovereign God who is working, and our peace must come from resting in that reality. Because God rules and controls all things, this theological consideration should lead to several expectations.

First, we should expect that God will be working through these situations, regardless of the outcome. God can certainly use sickness and affliction to bring about salvation. However, we must also have confidence that God can use sickness to mould and shape believers towards a heightened faithfulness when health returns. Baxter instructs us on how to nurture such an awakening: 'If they recover, be sure to remind them of their promises and resolutions in time of sickness. Go to them purposely to set these home to their consciences; and whenever, afterwards, you see them remiss, go to them, and put them in mind of what they said when they were stretched on a sickbed.'[6] Whether sickness leads to salvation, recovery or a sweeter fellowship with Jesus until death, remind them to remember that God is at work.

Second, we should expect that God will use us. In all our insensitivities, fumbled words and weaknesses that could make us painfully ineffective, God is all-powerful and will use us to fulfil his purposes. One of these purposes is to mould and shape us towards greater trust and dependence upon him. The sovereignty and goodness of God is magnified when we who visit are ministered to by afflicted and suffering Christians. If God in his infinitely wise plan ministers to us through the sick, surely God can and will use us and our weaknesses to minister to them.

Third, we should expect that God, by the power of the Holy Spirit, will give us the words to say. D. A. Carson captures a common apprehension as we wrestle with how to pray for others:

> What precisely should we be praying for with respect to each member of our family—and why? Someone close to us contracts a terminal disease: what should we pray for, and why? For healing? For freedom from pain? For faith and perseverance? For acceptance of what has befallen? And would it make a difference if the person in question were seventy-five years of age, as opposed to twenty-nine? Why, or why not? Are there some things we may humbly request from God and others we should boldly claim? If so, what kinds of things fall into each category?[7]

These are good questions to ask. At some point, however, we must trust in God's Word treasured in our hearts (Ps. 119:11), our love for the individual whom we are visiting and the sufficiency of his Spirit as we depend upon him for the words to say and pray.

Finally, we can expect that God will use all these things for the joy of his people and the glory of his name. What hope we have as Christians! Even in sickness and suffering, God will use it all for the joy of both the sick and the one who visits. In all this, God will work in such a way that he will be honoured above all else.

The driving purpose of all these theological considerations is God's glory. God is honoured when the things of God are prayed. God is honoured when his great character and ways are made known. God is honoured when the sick and those caring for them have an unshakable faith and trust that he is working for their good and for his glory. Regardless of how faithfully we walk according to these theological principles, our aim must be God's aim—our joy in God, our love of God's people and the glory of his great name. With this theological foundation in mind, let us move to pastoral considerations.

Pastoral
considerations

Even the stoutest sinners will hear us on their death-bed, though they scorned us before.

–Richard Baxter

A pastor is regularly faced with unique challenges. These are challenges that Scripture may not directly address but which will greatly affect those involved. In such moments, a pastor must exercise 'pastoral wisdom'. This is wisdom empowered by the Holy Spirit, wisdom that takes the clearly related teaching of Scripture on an issue and then acts in a manner that considers the practical ramifications of the action. In other words, pastoral wisdom is a bridge that often unites biblical doctrine to application in a unique situation.

Another such bridge that unites doctrine and application is preaching. The pastor's task is to connect the truth of Scripture and the application of it to the lives of his flock. The pastor's labour of study, prayer and meditation on both God's Word and his people is the bridge that unites doctrine and application when the church gathers publicly.

These considerations have both a theological as well as a practical element to them. Therefore, these pastoral considerations will be the bridges whereby we can connect the theological (Chapter 2) to the practical (Chapter 4). These considerations are pastoral in nature in that they do not just deal with the surface issues but reveal the heart, motive and attitude in which we carry them out.

Prepare your heart

Do not underestimate the intuition of the sick. We will often reveal by our manner whether we are going out of duty or love. This is the first heart issue we must honestly assess. It is an easy trap to fall into, especially for pastors. We begin to think that visiting is part of the job for which the church has hired us. Pastors must make a special effort to make sure that they are visiting the sick out of love and care, not obligation. Curtis Thomas, a seasoned American pastor of over forty years, writes, 'Our visits should never appear only as professional duties. If the patient perceives that we are there only to carry out our responsibility, rather than having a genuine concern for him or her, our visit can do more harm than good.'[8]

We must also prepare our hearts for what we might see and experience. Remember that we may be visiting someone who is close to dying and there are disturbing realities that accompany death. We may see blood or tubes and needles placed into unthinkable places. Deep pain, gasping of breath and many mannerisms can make even the toughest person squeamish. These circumstances are not, however, reasons to avoid going and caring for that person. In fact, these scenarios are wonderful moments that God gives to force us to prepare our hearts by relying completely on the Holy Spirit for strength.

We must prepare our hearts not just to avoid passing out when faced with these difficulties; we must prepare our hearts spiritually as well. Before we are face to face with the person we are visiting, we must have in mind the Scriptures we want to read. Think through which words of encouragement and hope you intend to bring. Whichever promises of God we choose to share, we should remind ourselves of them, believe them and allow them to fill our hearts with joy. That same intuition of the sick will then affirm to them that they are receiving words of truth from those whose hope is also found in them.

Watch your time

There are many wise thoughts on the issue of time. How long should we stay when we visit? Is it different depending on whom and where we visit? A helpful starting place is to consider the wise words of Alistair Begg: 'It is always better that people should feel our visit is too short than too long.'[9] With this in mind, most recommend no longer than five to ten minutes in a hospital or nursing home. If the sick are in hospital, it is a safe assumption that they are in some level of pain. Because of this, we care for them more faithfully by not 'pushing the line' by staying too long. A home situation can be a little more flexible. Depending on the level of sickness and pain of the individuals you are visiting, twenty to thirty minutes is plenty of time to spend with them.

How soon should we visit once we have received word of a person's illness? This is dependent upon the condition and affliction of the person. In the nineteenth century, people died of what today we think of as quite ordinary illnesses. This explains why David Dickson wrote, 'When the elder does hear of such illness, he should visit *at once*. A day's, or even an hour's, unnecessary delay may cause him a long regret' (his italics).[10] In the age of modern medicine, there is not the sense of urgency there was then. However, there are emergencies that, once we receive word of them, should become our top priority. As Dickson wrote, if we tarry and miss the passing of a dear brother or sister in Christ because of our procrastination, we too will experience unnecessary regret.

Listen, don't solve

Marriage is a wonderful gift from God that teaches us many things about ourselves and about men and women in general. One such thing is the striking difference between the ways in which men and women deal with problems. Men often want to conquer and solve, while women want to be loved and nurtured. Since men are notorious for trying to solve problems, we men need to learn a valuable lesson that our wives have so patiently tried to teach us. As helpful as our problem-solving gift is to our families, we must know when to utilize it and when to suppress it. Visiting the sick is one of the times when we should suppress it. In the discomfort of the moment, we can find ourselves explaining, in a thoughtful three-part thesis, how God is going to use this affliction in the life of the precious soul lying in the hospital bed. But this is neither loving nor pastoral. Dickson gives us a helpful alternative:

> In cases of sudden and severe affliction, we may be able to do little more than weep with them that weep (Romans 12:15), giving that afflicted some word from the merciful and faithful High Priest, and perhaps taking hold of the sufferer's hand—an act of sympathy that often has a wonderful power to calm and soothe in times of deep distress.[11]

Much like what we need to do with our wives, we need simply to listen and love. Too few words are much more profitable in these scenarios than too many. Those suffering from affliction and sickness will feel more loved by us if we sympathize, not rationalize. Therefore, listen, don't solve.

Leave a note

When I first started hospital visitations, I often found my efforts and time were used in vain. This was not because of bad visits but because I would not actually get to see the sick person. So I would leave and try to come back a few hours later, but would miss the person again. I found myself wasting valuable time driving back and forth, with my efforts continually being met with discouragement. Unfortunately, no one had told me this simple and obvious tactic: leave a note.

There will be numerous times when the people you have gone to visit will be unavailable. In hospitals, they may have been taken for tests on other floors. They may be unconscious. They may be with doctors or nurses and not taking visitors. In nursing homes, they may be taking part in activities or sleeping. In rehab centres, they leave their rooms to do therapy several times a day. Even when you go to a person's home, he or she may not be at home or able to get up and answer the door. Leaving a note in these kinds of scenarios has, in my experience, been a very helpful and fruitful solution. It communicates and accomplishes several aspects of care that you would have pursued had you been able to see them. Here is an example of the kind of simple handwritten note I leave:

> Dear _____,
>
> Sorry I [we] missed you. Know that I am praying for you and trusting God's sovereign plans and purposes for you in this difficult time. I talked with the nurse and will let the congregation know of your updated circumstances. Please let me know if there is any way I can serve you or your family through this time. You can reach me day or night on this number: _____.
>
> Grateful for you,
>
> Brian & [others with me]

A note lets the sick know that we took the time to come, we are praying for them, we want to serve them in any way we can, and that they are still connected to their local churches despite their circumstances. They can read these notes over and over again for their encouragement long after you have gone.

Enjoy the moment

The stress and anxiety that often accompany these scenarios can cause us to miss the joy that comes from them. As we visit, we must be mindful to enjoy all that God will accomplish for his glory. Here are a few ways in which we should anticipate God's providence.

We should see visiting the sick as a divine opportunity to care for those who may not care for us. Baxter encourages this view: 'Even the stoutest sinners will hear us on their death-bed, though they scorned us before.'[12] One of the hardest things to do is to love those who despise you, but that is what our Saviour has commanded for his followers (Matt. 5:44; Luke 6:35). A struggling relationship I had with an elderly lady in my church greatly improved after I visited her in hospital. Baxter's counsel is profound, and obedience to Jesus' command is expected. Enjoy what God does when you are faithful to this exhortation.

We should enjoy the opportunity to care for those who are hurting. There is a spiritual sensitivity that is continually present in affliction and suffering. There is a joy in caring for those who are most in need of care. This is a privilege that we only have while on earth. Dickson writes in regard to this privilege:

> It is our part ... to do what [angels] are not privileged to do—to sit beside a dying believer, to smooth his pillow, to moisten his lips, to remind him of the rod and staff that are ready for his help in the dark valley (Ps. 23:4), and to direct his dying eye to Jesus. All this is a precious service we cannot render in heaven, but only on earth.[13]

Caring for the sick and hurting is an honour that brings great joy to Christians, if we are mindful to enjoy it.

We need to enjoy the gift of seeing a real and unshakable faith in Christ. There is no better place to experience this than alongside suffering saints who anticipate meeting their Saviour in a matter of moments. The faith of Christians is magnified in suffering. We should therefore not only enjoy experiencing the gospel shining in suffering, but we should also rejoice to be witnesses of lives that end with rejoicing in the person and work of Christ as their only hope.

Finally, we need to enjoy how God moulds, shapes and teaches us through these experiences. This is one of the reasons I enjoy not just visiting the sick and dying but also leading funerals. Our hearts are wired to forget that death and sickness can fall on each of us at any moment and will fall on all of us eventually. Through caring for the sick and afflicted, we are reminded of the fragility of life and our closeness to eternity. We should enjoy these experiences that God gives us by his grace because they remind us as Christians about what really matters. Sitting at his bedside after watching his father take his last breath, John Piper wrote these words:

> I look you in the face and promise you with all my heart: Never will I forsake your gospel. O how you believed in hell and heaven and Christ and cross and blood and righteousness and faith and salvation and the Holy Spirit and the life of holiness and love. I rededicate myself, Daddy, to serve your great and glorious Lord Jesus with all my heart and with all my strength. You have not lived in vain. Your life goes on in thousands. I am glad to be one.[14]

Our twenty-first-century culture demands that we as Christians do all we can to set our minds on the things above (Col. 3:1). Visiting the sick and dying is a means God gloriously uses to accomplish this heavenly focus in our lives, and it should be embraced.

You don't have to be a pastor to think 'pastorally'. Pondering these kinds of considerations will build the bridge from the theological into the practical, and it is to these practical considerations that we now turn.

Practical considerations

So long as we have a world wherein there is sin, it is a mercy that it is a world wherein there is sickness.

–J. C. Ryle

Theological considerations should come before practical considerations. We must first understand biblical doctrine in order to apply it both properly and practically. However, this is not to diminish the reality of the unique challenges we face in our modern day in regard to visiting the sick. Because of these challenges, we must also firmly grasp and apply the practical issues for the theological and pastoral to be most effective. In other words, if we are not mindful of these practical aspects, we may fail to communicate the theological, which is where the hope of the gospel is found. For this reason, I offer these practical matters for your consideration.

Make eye contact

We rarely notice good, effective eye contact—that is, until we experience bad eye contact. Consider for a moment the importance of eye contact in casual conversation with someone. Good eye contact communicates interest in both the person and what is being said. Bad eye contact, however, communicates lack of interest, boredom and presumed tension between both parties. These principles are magnified in a hospital room. Good eye contact immediately communicates that you are interested and comfortable with the patient. If you are visiting people in hospitals or nursing homes, they are already sensitive about their appearance. They have tubes coming out of them, machines pumping medication into them, and they are not cosmetically prepared for visitors. Bad eye contact will only heighten their already-sensitive disposition towards their appearance. We should be disciplined with our eye contact in our conversations with others, especially when visiting those in such circumstances.

Touch with discernment

The effective use of physical touch is not dependent upon whether you are a 'touchy-feely' kind of person. Appropriate physical touch can often communicate a love and care that words cannot. Those who are sick can easily develop 'leprosy syndrome'. In the first century, leprosy was the disease that caused a person to be banished from the city limits and totally ostracized. Imagine what it must have felt like to be treated so badly and unlovingly, all because of a physical stigma. The sick, especially those in a hospital context, can develop this syndrome very easily. Therefore, one of the most effective ways to communicate love to those who are suffering is through appropriate physical touch, such as touching a hand, arm or foot when praying, giving a light hug, or physically helping them to move to a chair. These efforts break down walls of insecurity and can open greater opportunities of trust and ministry.

There is, however, a need for great wisdom, caution and discernment. The response that physical touch brings can be mixed. We must therefore assess several issues to know what is appropriate and what is not. The age, gender and type of relationship you have with the person determine how you should engage with him or her. For example, I am very comfortable holding the hand of the eighty-five-year-old widow whom I know very well and who sees me as her grandson. I am not comfortable, however, with physically touching a female church member who is close to me in age (whether married or single). Physical touch can be incredibly helpful or damaging when you visit. Be very wise with how you use it.

Be pleasant

My eighty-year-old grandmother who loves NBA basketball

once told me that her favourite basketball player was Dennis Rodman. Out of care for her, I felt it necessary cautiously to ask why. Her response was, 'Because he smiles all the time.' My uneasy reply was, 'He smiles a lot, Grandma?' 'Yes,' my grandmother answered back confidently. 'He must be having a good time. Why else would he be smiling so much?' In the midst of her naive assessment of one of the most disturbing bad boys in the history of sports, there was a lesson in this exchange, a lesson most of our mothers and grandmothers have tried to teach us but which we have rejected as insignificant. Smile. Be pleasant. Look as if you are enjoying yourself. Whether we like it or not, our demeanour affects everything. There are three specific physical disciplines that I would like to bring to your attention.

First is facial expression. Effective facial expression is not just about smiling, and it is certainly not about putting on a facade. It is about knowing ourselves. We all have a natural resting face. That is the facial expression we each make when totally relaxed. If you are like me and have a naturally serious expression, you will have to make a stronger effort than your friend who has been blessed with a naturally pleasant expression. The goal is to have a genuinely pleasant demeanour that communicates that you are glad to be there.

Second is your posture. It has long been noted that slouching during a job interview conveys a negative message to the interviewer. The same is true for visiting a sick person lying in bed. Make sure that you are aware of your posture. It can determine how interested you appear to the person you have come to visit.

Third is your manner of voice. Your vocal tone and inflection can be significant means of conveying either warmth and care or harshness and insensitivity. Dickson gives wise counsel: 'A low, quiet voice is usually soothing and pleasant to them, especially if they are weak and nervous. Don't let us strain them with anything requiring long or continuous attention.'[15] This principle becomes clearer as we consider the way in which babies respond to us. Even before they understand a word we say, infants are impacted by the tone of our voice. A loud and abrupt voice scares an infant, while a gentle and soothing voice produces smiles and coos. Our efforts are far from an exact science. We simply need to realize that our faces, voices and other physical expressions powerfully communicate long before one truth is uttered from our mouths.

Be perceptive

Regardless of where we are going to visit, we must be very aware of our surroundings. In a hospital room, we have not only a sick person lying in bed, but also IV lines, machine cords, oxygen lines, call buttons, blood pressure cuffs and a possible roommate or other members of the ward, who increase the intensity of the environment more than the previous aspects. We may also find other family members or doctors present. There is much for our observation, which cannot take place successfully unless we are mindful of these issues and make mental notes as we walk into a room.

We must also be aware of where we are when we speak to the sick. If possible, it is helpful to speak to them on the same level. In other words, instead of standing over them as they lie in bed, pull up a chair and position yourself at an equal level. This may seem a small thing, but it can prove to be less threatening. We should also be perceptive about the levels of pain they may be experiencing. This will be easier to detect if we have been thoughtful enough to plan ahead and find out their current condition. This is not difficult to know if they are in a hospital setting. We certainly cannot know all that is going on in the room and with the people we are visiting, but a little homework and awareness of our surroundings can make a vast difference in our comfort levels, as well as those of the people we are visiting.

Freshen your breath

Remember how you felt the last time you spoke with someone whose breath took your breath away? Consider how distracting and unpleasant it was. Consider what your impression of that person was after that encounter. Most of us find this issue to be deeply personal to us, and it is offensive and embarrassing if someone bothers to bring it to our attention. However, there is a simple solution for everyone: be humble and aware of it. Always carry with you gum or a mint to take care of the problem. Of all the things that can negatively affect our ministry to others, this one is, with a little awareness and planning, the easiest to eliminate.

Having considered this issue, we must also be gracious concerning the breath of those we are visiting. Even though you should expect your breath to be pleasant, it is an unrealistic expectation for sick people, who have not showered nor brushed their teeth in days, to be able to do anything about it. Therefore, be gracious and sensitive to their situations.

In summary, our efforts in these areas will benefit both parties involved. However, in the midst of what I hope will be helpful practical tips for more fruitful visitation, remember that it is God who causes the growth (1 Cor. 3:7). These practical suggestions must be approached with a complete dependence upon God's grace and Spirit. We must not be deceived into thinking that our own abilities in our own power produce spiritual fruit, lest we visit the sick with proud and self-sufficient hearts. In order to make our spiritual care of the sick more effective in our modern-day context, we must possess an awareness of these practical considerations.

Conclusion

During that epidemic of cholera, though I had many engagements in the country, I gave them up that I might remain in London to visit the sick and the dying.

–Charles Spurgeon

Charles Spurgeon is celebrated as one of the most gifted, dedicated, brilliant and effective preachers and pastors in history. This honourable distinction is given by most because of his piercing, articulate, Christ-centred and Word-driven sermons that were heard and have been read by thousands all over the world. Because of the popularity that Spurgeon reached in his ministry, his faithfulness as a very young pastor is often overlooked.

In 1854, at the age of just twenty, Spurgeon moved to pastor a church in London (New Park Street Chapel), which later became the Metropolitan Tabernacle. Spurgeon had been in London barely twelve months when a severe case of cholera swept through the city. Spurgeon recounted his efforts to care for and visit the numerous sick in the midst of horrific conditions:

> All day, and sometimes all night long, I went about from house to house, and saw men and women dying, and, oh, how glad they were to see my face! When many were afraid to enter their houses lest they should catch the deadly disease, we who had no fear about such things found ourselves most gladly listened to when we spoke of Christ and of things Divine.[16]

What an extraordinary example of a young, inexperienced pastor who feared God more than a contagious disease! What a model for each of us as we see the sacrificial care that Spurgeon gave at great risk because he knew of the spiritual fruit that could come only at the bedside of a dying man!

Spurgeon made visiting the afflicted a priority. Even as a young pastor, Spurgeon's gift of preaching was evident to all who heard him, which brought great demands on his time. Yet Spurgeon placed all those opportunities aside: 'During that epidemic of cholera, though I had many engagements in the country, I gave them up that I might remain in London to visit the sick and the dying.'[17] The demands on the life of Charles Spurgeon, even at twenty years of age, were great, quite possibly greater than the demands on most of us who live in one of the busiest cultures in history. We can certainly see through Spurgeon's example the significant impact that visiting the sick can have. However, what may be most applicable through this account are the sacrifices made by Spurgeon to make this divine task a priority. He emphasized that this priority was not only for pastors and leaders in the church, but 'for all who love souls'.[18]

Brothers and sisters in Christ, may we show our deep love for souls, specifically the souls of those with whom we have made a covenant in our local churches. As we fellowship with, love, care for and encourage one another, let us not lose sight of those who can easily be forgotten. Let us not forget those who do not fight for our attention like so many other things in our lives. We must take the initiative. Visiting the sick will not slide into our schedules. However, take heart. When we are deliberate about visiting the sick and afflicted in our churches, we can trust that a divine task is being done, souls are being loved and nurtured, we are being changed, the gospel is being revealed, and God is being glorified.

Afterword

Well, there you have it—finally a practical manual on how to visit the sick, primarily in the hospital setting, though these helpful points can be used in any setting. Brian has given all of us very instructive concepts. But the reality is that, unless the 'rubber meets the road', all of this effort has been for nothing more than intellectual gymnastics. Are you willing to stick your neck out?

Let me give you an example from the world of medicine in which I live. If a surgeon ever tells you that he has never taken out a normal, healthy appendix, you want to think twice before using his services. The task of diagnosing appendicitis is ultimately not that exact. If he has never taken out a normal appendix, he has probably missed a few cases of appendicitis. Likewise, when you visit the sick, if you do not delve into the uncertain waters of gospel presentation, you will never get 'shot down'. Just like the surgeon who may infrequently take out a normal appendix, your efforts may not go as hoped. Which do you think is more important: your ego or being faithful to our Lord's command to share the gospel and comfort the sick? I believe Brian has given us very useful tools. I encourage you to use them. The proverbial ball is now in your court.

A very blessed dad,
Bill Croft

A note to pastors

This book is not just for you. Though I had you on my mind through much of its development, this work is intended to have a much broader purpose. It is to be used to deliberately train and equip the people of your congregation in this task of visiting the sick. My prayer is that you will not only be challenged by the exhortation to visit the sick personally, but also that you will be convicted to train your people to do likewise. I want, therefore, to commend five ways in which you can effectively teach, train and motivate your people to see the value in caring for the afflicted and dying within your local church.

Exhort through preaching

As you are committed to preaching the Bible, look for those points of application that serve as exhortations to love, care for and serve the afflicted in your church. Refer back to the chapter on biblical considerations for assistance. Regardless of where in the Bible you are preaching in a particular week, you will find a sovereign God who is ruling over the afflictions and sufferings of people. You will see God's glory displayed as his people care for those in need for the sake of the gospel. This is one reason why expositional preaching is the most helpful steady diet for a local church. As you preach through books of the Bible, you are more likely to be confronted with texts that allow this type of instruction. However, there is nothing wrong with making this topic the basis for a short sermon series when appropriate. But regardless of how you teach your congregation about visiting the sick—whether through a short sermon series or through regular application in your expositional sermons—the preaching of the Word of God is that which gives life to the church, and it is where we are able to exhort with authority that which is most important to the entire body. Show the care of the sick and afflicted as a priority by exhorting through public preaching.

Pray for the afflicted in public gatherings

I will admit that praying the never-ending prayer list when the church gathers can turn into a meaningless, painful mantra. This is not what I am proposing. I am encouraging you to pick a couple of significant afflictions in your church that you can highlight through public prayer for the purposes of informing and teaching your congregation how we should face these struggles. Praying for these serious situations informs the congregation about what is going on, but it also allows you to teach your congregation how to face these difficulties by the way you pray publicly.

When you pray, pray specific biblical truths. Praise God for his sovereign power over sickness and death. Thank God for the hope we have of physical wholeness and resurrection one day because of Christ. Pray for healing if it be God's will to heal. Pray for the gospel to be known in the lives of those who are suffering as Christ is magnified in our weakness. Pray for the medical personnel caring for them, yet recognizing God as the great healer. Then pray that the gospel would be seen in your faithful care, as a local church, of those enduring these afflictions. Seize the public gatherings of the church to pray for these needs, as not only are they wonderful moments for teaching and motivating, but also there is great power in corporate intercession.

Inform your people regularly

Willing church members are more likely to serve the sick and afflicted if they know what is going on and where to go. Lack of knowledge can be very discouraging for someone who wants to help but does not know how to gather the appropriate information. Create a system within your local church so that members can be informed and updated regularly as circumstances develop and change. Bulletins and prayer chains have been an effective way to get the word out in the past and can still be useful now. Church-wide email appears to be the trend for the future. Whatever the method, be committed to keeping your people updated, not just on the circumstances to know how to pray better, but also with the information they need to go and physically visit and care for those struggling. Hospital and room numbers; whether they want visitors; how close someone may be to dying; and particular things that church members can go and do for them: these are just a few specific details that are helpful for those who are more detached from the daily grind of pastoral labour. Busy church members can find endless reasons not to bother with caring for the sick. Let us not allow being uninformed to be one of them.

Lead by example

We cannot expect our people to be faithful in this task if we are not. The obvious truth of this in our lives does not give us the luxury of dismissing it. We can preach on caring for the sick, we can pray in every public gathering for them, we can give detailed assessments of the daily needs of the afflicted, but if we are not engaged in visiting the sick ourselves and our congregations are not affected by our efforts, we have failed. A soldier is more willing to follow his general into battle than to charge upon his command from a distant post. Fellow pastors, we must not only visit but must also model a burden for the sick and afflicted for our people. We must model a great faith in our sovereign God and a tender fellowship with our Saviour in these moments, knowing that he works all things for his own glory and for the good of his people. Lead faithfully in this way, and your people will follow.

Publicly lift up the example of others

A model of care for the sick doesn't have to come solely from you. Seize key opportunities to praise and lift up lay people in your church who faithfully care for the afflicted and dying. For example, on Wednesday evenings in my church, we have a time of informally sharing what we are thankful for. I will use this time to highlight a faithful brother or sister who has sacrificially cared for a dying member that week and give thanks for his or her effort and faithfulness. As you lift up those who are faithful in visiting the afflicted, God often will use those examples to move others to do the same.

My fellow labourers in the gospel, this book is intended to aid our faithful shepherding of our flocks. Yet it is also to be used to teach the members of our flocks to care for one another. May God use the platform he has given us to urge others to care for the sick, and may he use all our labour for his good purposes and for the glory of his great name.

Appendix 1: Checklist

Take this list with you and review it before you make your visits.

Theological

- Ask leading questions
- Read Scripture
- Pray the gospel
- Affirm the promises and attributes of God
- Trust God's sovereign plan

Pastoral

- Prepare your heart
- Watch your time
- Listen, don't solve
- Leave a note
- Enjoy the moment

Practical

- Make eye contact
- Touch with discernment
- Be pleasant
- Be perceptive
- Freshen your breath

Appendix 2: Spiritual conversation

Pastor–patient conversation

This is an example of a conversation between a pastor and patient in a hospital room that moves from 'small talk' and physical issues to more spiritual matters.[19] Please realize that this is one of many possible scenarios depending upon the answers given by the individual. I pray that this example will at least encourage you to see the value of thinking about these prospective opportunities before you find yourself in them.

Pastor: I have been enjoying our conversation, but can I put you on the spot and ask you a personal question?

Patient: Uh, yeah, I guess so.

Pastor: In light of your physical condition, have you considered what happens to each of us when we die?

Patient: Yes, I have begun to think about that more and more.

Pastor: Are you ready to die and stand before God?

Patient: I don't know. I hope so.

Pastor: Why do you believe God would allow you into heaven?

Patient: I've lived a pretty good life ... I'm a good person.

Pastor: Are you interested in hearing what the Bible says about this?

Patient: Yes, I think I would like to know.

Pastor: The Bible teaches that God is eternally holy, righteous and perfect in all his ways (Ps. 145). God created the world and it was good and perfect, including man, who was made in God's image (Gen. 1–2). Yet when Adam and Eve sinned and rebelled against God's commands, they brought sin into the world, which eternally separated them from God (Gen. 3). The consequence of sin being in the world is that we, as Adam's descendents, are now born into sin and are thus guilty of rebellion against God (Rom. 5:12). Another consequence of this sinfulness is that God, in his holy and righteous character, must punish sin by death

(Rom. 6:23), and as a result we are described as objects of his wrath and judgement (Eph. 2:3).

However, the Bible also teaches that God is rich in mercy (Eph. 2:4) and, in his amazing love for sinners, provided a way for us not only to escape his judgement but also to be eternally reconciled with him (2 Cor. 5:18). All this was accomplished by his own Son, Jesus, who was born a human just like us (Phil. 2:8). Although he lived a perfect, sinless life, he died on the cross. On the cross, God accomplished his reconciling purpose as his own Son bore the full wrath and judgement of God in our place (2 Cor. 5:21). He rose from the dead three days later, conquering death and providing us life through him (Rom. 4:25). Through Jesus, we not only have forgiveness of our sins (Col. 1:14), but we also have his righteousness given to us so that we can stand blameless before God (2 Cor. 5:21). We receive this, not by anything we have done, but through faith in who Jesus is and the work he accomplished on the cross, shedding his own blood on our behalf (Rom. 5:8–10). We must simply acknowledge our sin and rebellion against God, see that Jesus is the one who sufficiently paid our penalty for sin (Heb. 10:12), repent (turn) from our sins, and by faith alone trust in Jesus (Mark 1:15). Have you ever heard this before? How does this strike you?

Patient: Well, I would like to think about what you have shared with me. Is there a way I can reach you if I have some questions?

Pastor: Sure. [Give mobile phone number.] You know, this is a very appropriate time in your life to consider these issues seriously. Do you mind if I pray with you?

Patient: No, I would like that.

Doctor–patient conversation

This is a more conversational example of how my father, a Christian physician who has practised medicine for over thirty years, typically attempts to accomplish this same objective.

Doctor: John, can I put you on the spot?

Patient: I guess so.

Doctor: All of us will face death at some time. But your 'condition' will require you to look at death sooner than some. When you die, do you think you will go to heaven?

Patient: I think so [or hope so]. [If this response is given, you know that the patient either cannot verbalize the gospel or does not know it at all.]

Doctor: John, when you stand before the Lord and he says, 'John, why should I let you into heaven?' what would be your response?

Patient: Well, I've been a good person.

Doctor: John, let me give you a few issues to consider. If I were to ask you the characteristics of God, you would probably respond with the fact that God is loving, holy, all-knowing, all-powerful, kind, and so forth. But the characteristic that gets you and me into trouble is that God is just.

Because of God's perfect justice, neither you nor I can spend eternity with a just and holy God if we have ever committed sin. There is an old saying that rings all too true: 'Good people don't go to heaven; forgiven people go to heaven.' God, in his great mercy, has made a way for sinners like you and me to be forgiven. When Christ came into the world, he had two main purposes: first, to show us a glimpse of who God is; second, to provide a way for sinners to be reconciled to God and to be forgiven by him.

When Christ died on the cross, he bore the punishment for the sins of all who would confess their state as sinners and accept Jesus by faith alone as their Saviour and Lord. He paid the price for our sin. At the moment we turn from sin and trust Christ, our sins are forgiven and God sees us as though we have the righteousness of Christ. This is the great exchange: my sinfulness for his righteousness.

So the answer to the question about why Christ should let you into heaven has nothing to do with what we do. It has everything to do with what Christ did for us if we have accepted his offer of forgiveness. Has there ever been a time in your life when you confessed your sins and trusted in Jesus?

Patient: [One possible response.] Yes, I have.

Doctor: Can you tell me about it? [Take it from here.]

Or:

Patient: [Another possible response.] No, there has not.

Doctor: It is not my intention to coerce you into a decision. If you want, I will help you in the process of accepting Christ. If you would like to ponder these things further, you should feel free to do so.

[Then follow up as appropriate if you determine that the patient is a Christian.]

Doctor: John, you probably have known all that I have told you but were just unable to verbalize these truths in a particular way. When I first asked you about going to heaven, you had an 'I hope so' response. It is so very important for you as a Christian to know that you are guaranteed that you will go to heaven when you die. That assurance will be a foundational truth you will want to hold onto as your 'condition' progresses. Read the first eleven verses of Ephesians 1 and rest on the assurance that Christ, through the apostle Paul, gives us. If you have further questions, please contact me.

Appendix 3: FAQ

Here are ten frequently asked questions that were not addressed in the body of this book but are important issues that should be thoughtfully considered.

1. When is it appropriate for children to participate in visits?

When appropriate, the participation of children should be embraced. Children can lift the spirits of a lonely, hurting person in ways our best efforts cannot. Children's participation can also be a wonderful tool in training them to care for people in our churches. There are many times, however, when children should not go with you to visit. Here are a few of those scenarios: a patient has a condition with intense pain; a patient is in a section of the hospital where infections passed on can be harmful to the patient (e.g. ICU); a home-bound person is uncomfortable around children. These are just a few factors to consider in making a wise decision. Ultimately, prayerful discernment and wisdom are needed. When unsure, it is best to err on the safe side, knowing that there will be other opportunities for training and including your children in your labour.

2. Can music and/or singing be an effective way to care for the sick?

Yes, but only if you are gifted to do so. We don't want a sincere, well-meaning but 'tone-deaf' visitor to bring more misery upon sick individuals. However, there are many times when it is appropriate to use music to lift spirits, soothe aches and communicate biblical truth. It is important to proceed with sensitivity to the environment; for example, don't bring cymbals into a hospital room. However, taking a group of members from church to a nursing home to sing Christmas carols at Christmas time is very appropriate and meaningful for both the singers and the hearers.

3. How do I relate to other family members who are in the hospital room?

It is important that we always introduce ourselves to all in the room and treat them with kindness and respect. If the patient is asleep or unconscious, others in the room can provide an update on the patient's condition. We could also find ourselves with an opportunity to minister to the family and friends present. We do need to make sure, however, that our main focus is always on the patient. Even if we are talking with family members, our main topic of conversation needs to be the sick individual we came to visit.

4. What should I wear to visit someone who is in hospital?

Use good judgement and common sense. Always take into consideration the person you are visiting and what will be comfortable for him or her. Those from an older generation may want us to be more formal, while those from a younger generation may desire more informal attire. A safe middle ground is 'business casual'. It is wise to be thoughtful about this issue, but we can become obsessed with it to the point that we make our decisions based on the fear of man.

5. At what time of day should most visits take place?

We should try to honour the visiting hours of a hospital if at all possible. When that is not an option, we need to determine how important it is that we go to visit before another appropriate time may come. Although patients in hospitals sleep on and off throughout the day, avoid exceptionally early or late visits. This is a good general rule for hospitals and homes alike.

6. How do I lead into a spiritual conversation?
See Appendix 2.

7. How do I find a person's ward or room in a hospital or nursing home?

You can generally phone the hospital and find out in which ward or room the patient is staying. Otherwise, once you get to the hospital or nursing home, find the information desk. The staff there can not only give you the room number but can also direct you along the quickest and easiest route for finding it. Hospitals can be very overwhelming, especially for those who are not often in them. Therefore, don't be embarrassed to ask for help or assistance. It is a way to cultivate humility and use the resources of the hospital.

8. When is it appropriate to take someone with me?

If you think that the person to accompany you will be a help during the visit rather than a hindrance, it will be appropriate to take the person in most cases. Having said that, a better question might be, 'When *should* I take someone with me?' Some great reasons to bring someone along are: training purposes, discomfort from going by yourself, fellowship purposes, or the need for a second person for the sake of accountability. If you do take someone with you, you should take advantage of having someone to observe you in that environment. We need to be intentional about evaluating our efforts so that we can learn how to be most effective.

9. How can I be respectful to the nurses and medical staff caring for the people I come to visit?

It is tempting to bypass the nurse's station when coming to visit, especially if we recently acquired the patient's updated information and room number. However, reflecting the gospel as we visit is not accomplished solely in the room with the patient but also with those we encounter along the way. A good policy, therefore, is to stop by the nurse's station, if for no other reason than to introduce yourself to the nurses caring for the one you have come to visit. Ask how the patient is doing and if there is any updated information they can share about that person's condition. Privacy laws prevent nurses from sharing very much. However, by waiting patiently and speaking kindly to them, we affirm their authority and role in the care of the patient. This communicates respect, affirms them in their labour and, most importantly, conveys a helpful picture of the gospel when we introduce ourselves as a pastor, deacon or fellow church member of the patient.

10. How do I approach visiting someone who is sharing a room with other patients?

Though a semi-private room is frequently seen as an inconvenience, we should recognize it as a great opportunity. We must always be polite, respectful and sensitive so that we do not disturb other patients when attempting to see those we have come to visit. Nevertheless, always assume the attentiveness of other people in the room when we visit. All the Scriptures, prayers, kind words, truths of the gospel and hopeful promises of God we share with those we have come to visit will be heard by these other patients. The power of the Holy Spirit can reveal the truth of the gospel to other patients as well as to those whom we are directly visiting and addressing. As you leave, use pastoral wisdom to discern whether God has provided an opportunity to minister to other patients.

Appendix 4: 'Sickness'

by J. C. Ryle (abridged version)

John Charles Ryle was born on 10 May 1816 and is arguably the best-known and most influential Anglican bishop of the nineteenth century. Ryle is most celebrated for his uncompromising convictions, faithful exposition of Scripture, powerful Christ-centred preaching, diligence in his pastoral work and clarity in his writing. Since his death on 10 June 1900, Ryle has continued to be a profound voice for the edification of the church and the furtherance of the gospel. The following paper, Sickness, was written by Ryle to pursue that purpose. He approaches this topic in a biblically faithful, pastoral and thoughtful manner, and the inclusion of this paper here brings a historical coherence. Read his heart on this matter, be challenged, and may it lead to a proper understanding of sickness so that you will be fully equipped to care for the sick to the glory of God. I strongly commend this work for your consideration.

He whom You love is sick.

–John 11:3

The chapter from which this text is taken is well known to all Bible readers. In life-like description, in touching interest, in sublime simplicity, there is no writing in existence that will bear comparison with that chapter. A narrative like this is to my own mind one of the great proofs of the inspiration of Scripture. When I read the story of Bethany, I feel, 'There is something here which the infidel can never account for. This is nothing else but the finger of God.'

The words which I specially dwell upon in this chapter are singularly affecting and instructive. They record the message which Martha and Mary sent to Jesus when their brother Lazarus was sick: 'Lord, behold, he whom You love is sick.' That message was short and simple. Yet almost every word is deeply suggestive.

I invite the attention of my readers to the subject of sickness. The subject is one which we ought frequently to look in the face. We cannot avoid it. It needs no prophet's eye to see sickness coming to each of us in turn one day. 'In the midst of life we are in death.' Let us turn aside for a few moments, and consider sickness as Christians. The consideration will not hasten its coming, and by God's blessing may teach us wisdom.

In considering the subject of sickness, three points appear to me to demand attention. On each I shall say a few words.

- The universal prevalence of sickness and disease.
- The general benefits which sickness confers on mankind.
- The special duties to which sickness calls us.

1. The universal prevalence of sickness

I need not dwell long on this point. To elaborate the proof of it would only be multiplying truisms, and heaping up common-places which all allow. Sickness is everywhere. In Europe, in Asia, in Africa, in America; in hot countries and in cold, in civilized nations and in savage tribes—men, women and children sicken and die.

Sickness is among all classes. Grace does not lift a believer above the reach of it. Riches will not buy exemption from it. Rank cannot prevent its assaults. Kings and their subjects, masters and servants, rich men and poor, learned and unlearned, teachers and scholars, doctors and patients, ministers and hearers, all alike go down before this great foe. 'A rich man's wealth is his strong city' (Prov. 18:11). The Englishman's house is called his castle; but there are no doors and bars which can keep out disease and death.

Sickness is not preventable by anything that man can do. The average duration of life may doubtless be somewhat lengthened. The skill of doctors may continually discover new remedies, and effect surprising cures. The enforcement of wise sanitary regulations may greatly lower the death-rate in a land. But, after all, whether in healthy or unhealthy localities, whether in mild climates or in cold, whether treated by homeopathy or allopathy, men will sicken and die. 'As for the days of our life, they contain seventy years, or if due to strength, eighty years, Yet their pride is but labor and sorrow; for soon it is gone and we fly away' (Ps. 90:10). That witness is indeed true. It was true 3,300 years ago. It is true still.

The universal prevalence of sickness is one of the indirect evidences that the Bible is true. The Bible explains it. The Bible answers the questions about it which will arise in every inquiring mind. No other systems of religion can do this. They all fail here. They are silent. They are confounded. The Bible alone looks the subject in the face. It boldly proclaims the fact that man is a fallen creature, and with equal boldness proclaims a vast remedial system to meet his wants. I feel shut up to the conclusion that the Bible is from God. Christianity is a revelation from heaven. 'Your word is truth' (John 17:17).

2. The general benefits which sickness confers on mankind

I use that word 'benefits' advisedly. I feel it of deep importance to see this part of our subject clearly. I know well that sickness is one of the supposed weak points in God's government of the world, on which sceptical minds love to dwell. 'Can God be a God of love, when he allows pain? Can God be a God of mercy, when he permits disease? He might prevent pain and disease; but he does not. How can these things be?' Such is the reasoning which often comes across the heart of man.

I know the suffering and pain which sickness entails. I admit the misery and wretchedness which it often brings in its train. But I cannot regard it as an unmixed evil. I see in it a wise permission of God. I see in it a useful provision to check the ravages of sin and the devil among men's souls. If man had never sinned I should have been at a loss to discern the benefit of sickness. But since sin is in the world, I can see that sickness is a good. It is a blessing quite as much as a curse. It is a rough schoolmaster, I grant. But it is a real friend to man's soul.

Sickness helps to remind men of death. The most live as if they were never going to die. They follow business, or pleasure, or politics or science, as if earth was their eternal home. They plan and scheme for the future, like the rich fool in the parable, as if they had a long lease of life, and were not tenants at will. A heavy illness sometimes goes far to dispel these delusions. It awakens men from their daydreams, and reminds them that they have to die as well as to live. Now this I say emphatically is a mighty good.

Sickness helps to make men think seriously of God, and their souls, and the world to come. The most in their days of health can find no time for such thoughts. They dislike them. They put them away. They count them troublesome and disagreeable. Now a severe disease has sometimes a wonderful power of mustering and rallying these thoughts, and bringing them up before the eyes of a man's soul. Even a wicked king like Ben-hadad, when sick, could think of Elisha (2 Kings 8:8). Even heathen sailors, when death was in sight, were afraid, and cried every man to his god (Jonah 1:5). Surely anything that helps to make men think is a good.

Sickness helps to soften men's hearts, and teach them wisdom. The natural heart is as hard as a stone. It can see no good in anything which is not of this life, and no happiness excepting in this world. A long illness sometimes goes far to correct these ideas. It exposes the emptiness and hollowness of what the world calls 'good' things, and teaches us to hold them with a loose hand. The man of business finds that money alone is not everything the heart requires. The woman of the world finds that costly apparel, and novel-reading, and the reports of balls and operas, are miserable comforters in a sick room. Surely anything that obliges us to alter our weights and measures of earthly things is a real good.

Sickness helps to level and humble us. We are all naturally proud and high-minded. Few, even of the poorest, are free from the infection. Few are to be found who do not look down on somebody else, and secretly flatter themselves that they are 'not as other men'. A sickbed is a mighty tamer of such thoughts as these. It forces on us the mighty truth that we are all poor worms that we 'dwell in houses of clay', and are 'crushed before the moth' (Job 4:19), and that kings and subjects, masters and servants, rich and poor, are all dying creatures, and will soon stand side by side at the bar of God. In the sight of the coffin and the grave it is not easy to be proud. Surely anything that teaches that lesson is good.

Finally, sickness helps to try men's religion, of what sort it is. There are not many on earth who have no religion at all. Yet few have a religion that will bear inspection. Most are content with traditions received from their fathers, and can render no reason of the hope that is in them. Now disease is sometimes most useful to a man in exposing the utter worthlessness of his soul's foundation. It often shows him that he has nothing solid under his feet, and nothing firm under his hand. It makes him find out that, although he may have had a form of religion, he has been all his life worshipping 'an unknown God'. Surely anything that makes us find out the real character of our faith is a good.

We have no right to murmur at sickness and repine at its presence in the world. We ought rather to thank God for it. It is God's witness. It is the soul's adviser. It is an awakener to the conscience. It is a purifier to the heart. Surely I have a right to tell you that sickness is a blessing and not a curse, a help and not an injury, a gain and not a loss, a friend and not a foe to mankind. So long as we have a world wherein there is sin, it is a mercy that it is a world wherein there is sickness.

3. The special duties to which the prevalence of sickness calls on us

I should be sorry to leave the subject of sickness without saying something on this point. I hold it to be of cardinal importance not to be content with generalities in delivering God's message to souls. I am anxious to impress on each one into whose hands this paper may fall, his own personal responsibility in connection with the subject. I would fain have no one lay down this paper unable to answer the questions, 'What practical lesson have I learned? What, in a world of disease and death, what ought I to do?'

One paramount duty which the prevalence of sickness entails on man is that of living habitually prepared to meet God. Sickness is a remembrancer of death. Death is the door through which we must all pass to judgement. Judgement is the time when we must at last see God face to face. Surely the first lesson which the inhabitant of a sick and dying world should learn should be to prepare to meet his God.

I believe that this, and nothing less than this, is preparedness to meet God. Pardon of sin and meetness for God's presence, justification by faith and sanctification of the heart, the blood of Christ sprinkled on us, and the Spirit of Christ dwelling in us: these are the grand essentials of the Christian religion. These are no mere words and names to furnish bones of contention for wrangling theologians. These are sober, solid, substantial realities. To live in the actual possession of these things, in a world full of sickness and death, is the first duty which I press home upon your soul.

Another paramount duty which the prevalence of sickness entails on you is that of living habitually ready to bear it patiently. Sickness is no doubt a trying thing to flesh and blood. To feel our nerves unstrung and our natural force abated, to be obliged to sit still and be cut off from all our usual avocations, to see our plans broken off and our purposes disappointed, to endure long hours, and days, and nights of weariness and pain, all this is a severe strain on poor sinful human nature. What wonder if peevishness and impatience are brought out by disease! Surely in such a dying world as this we should study patience.

One more paramount duty which the prevalence of sickness entails on you is that of habitual readiness to feel with and help your fellow men. Sickness is never very far from us. Few are the families who have not some sick relative. Few are the parishes where you will not find someone ill. But wherever there is sickness, there is a call to duty. A little timely assistance in some cases, a kindly visit in others, a friendly inquiry, a mere expression of sympathy, may do a vast good. These are the sorts of things which soften asperities, and bring men together, and promote good feeling. These are ways by which you may ultimately lead men to Christ and save their souls. These are good works to which every professing Christian should be ready. In a world full of sickness and disease we ought to 'Bear one another's burdens' and 'Be kind to one another' (Gal. 6:2; Eph. 4:32). If you can live in a sick and dying world and not feel for others, you have yet much to learn.

Practical application

And now I conclude all with four words of practical application. I want the subject of this paper to be turned to some spiritual use. My heart's desire and prayer to God in placing it in this volume is to do good to souls.

(1) In the first place, I offer a question to all who read this paper, to which, as God's ambassador, I entreat their serious attention. It is a question which grows naturally out of the subject on which I have been writing. It is a question which concerns all, of every rank, and class, and condition. I ask you, What will you do when you are ill? The time must come when you, as well as others, must go down the dark valley of the shadow of death. The hour must come when you, like all your forefathers, must sicken and die. The time may be near or

far off. God only knows. But whenever the time may be, I ask again, What are you going to do? Where do you mean to turn for comfort? On what do you mean to rest your soul? On what do you mean to build your hope? From whence will you fetch your consolations?

(2) In the next place, I offer counsel to all who feel they need it and are willing to take it, to all who feel they are not yet prepared to meet God. That counsel is short and simple. Acquaint yourself with the Lord Jesus Christ without delay. Repent, be converted, flee to Christ, and be saved. Either you have a soul or you have not. You will surely never deny that you have. Then if you have a soul, seek that soul's salvation. Of all gambling in the world, there is none so reckless as that of the man who lives unprepared to meet God, and yet puts off repentance. Either you have sins or you have not. If you have (and who will dare to deny it?), break off from those sins, cast away your transgressions, and turn away from them without delay. Either you need a Saviour or you do not.

Vague, and indefinite, and indistinct religion may do very well in time of health. It will never do in the day of sickness. A mere formal, perfunctory Church membership may carry a man through the sunshine of youth and prosperity. It will break down entirely when death is in sight. Nothing will do then but real heart-union with Christ. Christ interceding for us at God's right hand—Christ known and believed as our Priest, our Physician, our Friend—Christ alone can rob death of its sting and enable us to face sickness without fear. He alone can deliver those who through fear of death are in bondage. I say to everyone who wants advice, Be acquainted with Christ. As ever you would have hope and comfort on the bed of sickness, be acquainted with Christ. Seek Christ. Apply to Christ.

(3) In the third place, I exhort all true Christians who read this paper to remember how much they may glorify God in the time of sickness, and to lie quiet in quiet in God's hand when they are

ill. I earnestly entreat all sick believers to remember that they may honour God as much by patient suffering as they can by active work. It often shows more grace to sit still than it does to go to and fro, and perform great exploits. I entreat them to remember that Christ cares for them as much when they are sick as he does when they are well, and that the very chastisement they feel so acutely is sent in love, and not in anger.

Above all, I entreat them to recollect the sympathy of Jesus for all his weak members. They are always tenderly cared for by him, but never so much as in their time of need. Christ has had great experience of sickness. He knows the heart of a sick man. He used to see 'all manner of sickness, and all manner of disease' when he was upon earth. He felt specially for the sick in the days of his flesh. He feels for them specially still. Sickness and suffering, I often think, make believers more like their Lord in experience, than health. 'He Himself took our infirmities and carried away our diseases' (Matt. 8:17). The Lord Jesus was a 'man of sorrows and acquainted with grief' (Isa. 53:3). None have such an opportunity of learning the mind of a suffering Saviour as suffering disciples.

(4) I conclude with a word of exhortation to all believers, which I heartily pray God to impress upon their souls. I exhort you to keep up a habit of close communion with Christ, and never to be afraid of 'going too far' in your religion. Remember this, if you wish to have 'great peace' in your times of sickness. If you and I want 'strong consolation' in our time of need, we must not be content with a bare union with Christ (Heb. 6:18). We must seek to know something of heartfelt, experimental communion with him. Never, never let us forget, that 'union' is one thing, and 'communion' another. Thousands, I fear, who know what 'union' with Christ is, know nothing of 'communion'.

The day may come when after a long fight with disease, we shall feel that medicine can do no more, and that nothing remains but to die. Friends will be standing by, unable to help us. Hearing, eyesight, even the power of praying, will be fast failing us. The world and its shadows will be melting beneath our feet. Eternity, with its realities, will be looming large before our minds. What shall support us in that trying hour? What shall enable us to feel, 'I fear no evil' (Ps. 23:4)? Nothing, nothing can do it but close communion with Christ. Christ dwelling in our hearts by faith, Christ putting his right arm under our heads, Christ felt to be sitting by our side, Christ can alone give us the complete victory in the last struggle.

Let us cleave to Christ more closely, love him more heartily, live to him more thoroughly, copy him more exactly, confess him more boldly, follow him more fully. Religion like this will always bring its own reward. Worldly people may laugh at it. Weak brethren may think it extreme. But it will wear well. At even time it will bring us light. In sickness it will bring us peace. In the world to come it will give us a crown of glory that fadeth not away.

In the meantime let us live the life of faith in the Son of God. Let us lean all our weight on Christ, and rejoice in the thought that he lives for evermore. Yes, blessed be God! Christ lives, though we may die. Christ lives, though friends and families are carried to the grave. He lives who abolished death, and brought life and immortality to light by the gospel. He lives who said, 'Shall I ransom them from the power of Sheol? Shall I redeem them from death?' (Hosea 13:14). He lives who will one day change our vile body, and make it like unto his glorious body. In sickness and in health, in life and in death, let us lean confidently on him. Surely we ought to say daily with one of old, 'Blessed be God for Jesus Christ!'

FOR FURTHER INFORMATION AND HELP

Books

Baxter, Richard, *The Reformed Pastor*, ed. William Brown (Edinburgh: Banner of Truth, 2001)

Carson, D. A., *A Call to Spiritual Reformation: Priorities from Paul and His Prayers* (Grand Rapids, MI: Baker Books, 1992)

Dickson, David, *The Elder and His Work*, ed. George Kennedy McFarland and Philip Graham Ryken (Phillipsburg, NJ: P & R Publishing, 2004)

Prime, Derek, and Begg, Alistair, *On Being a Pastor: Understanding Our Calling and Work* (Chicago: Moody Publishers, 2004)

Spurgeon, C. H., *An All Round Ministry* (Edinburgh: Banner of Truth, 1960)

Spurgeon, C. H., Spurgeon, Susannah, and Harrald, W. J., *C. H. Spurgeon's Autobiography*, vol. i (Pasadena, TX: Pilgrim Publications, 1992)

Thomas, Curtis, *Practical Wisdom for Pastors: Words of Encouragement and Counsel for a Lifetime of Ministry* (Wheaton, IL: Crossway, 2001)

Websites

John Piper, 'Hello, My Father Just Died', posted 6 March 2007 at http://www.desiringgod.org/ ResourceLibrary/TasteAndSee/ ByDate/2007/2013/

Don Whitney, 'Ten Questions to Ask to Turn a Conversation Toward the Gospel', http://biblicalspirituality.org/gospelq.html

Thabiti Anyabwile's blog 'Pure Church': www.purechurch. blogspot.com

Ray Van Neste's blog 'Oversight of Souls': www.rvanneste. blogspot.com

ENDNOTES

1   Richard Baxter, *The Reformed Pastor*, ed. William Brown (Edinburgh: Banner of Truth, 2001), p. 102.

2   Charles Haddon Spurgeon, *An All Round Ministry* (Edinburgh: Banner of Truth, 1960), p. 384.

3   David Dickson, *The Elder and His Work*, ed. George Kennedy McFarland and Philip Graham Ryken (Phillipsburg, NJ: P & R Publishing, 2004), p. 58.

4   Ibid., p. 59.

5   This question *must* be followed up with some type of 'why' question. For example, 'Why do you believe God would allow you into heaven?' Answers that resemble 'Because I've been a good person/God is loving/I was baptized/I hope [think] so' reveal that they do not know the gospel. You must assess this first in order to be able to direct the rest of a spiritual conversation accordingly. See Appendix 2.

6   Baxter, *The Reformed Pastor*, p. 104.

7   D. A. Carson, *A Call to Spiritual Reformation: Priorities from Paul and His Prayers* (Grand Rapids, MI: Baker Books, 1992), p. 33.

8   Curtis Thomas, *Practical Wisdom for Pastors: Words of Encouragement and Counsel for a Lifetime of Ministry* (Wheaton, IL: Crossway, 2001), p. 104.

9   Derek Prime and Alistair Begg, *On Being a Pastor: Understanding Our Calling and Work* (Chicago: Moody Publishers, 2004), p. 175.

10   Dickson, *The Elder and His Work*, p. 60.

11   Ibid.

12   Baxter, *The Reformed Pastor*, p. 103.

13   Dickson, *The Elder and His Work*, pp. 60–61.

14   John Piper, 'Hello, My Father Just Died', posted 6 March 2007 at http://www.desiringgod.org/ResourceLibrary/TasteAndSee/ByDate/2007/2013_Hello_My_Father_Just_Died/ (accessed 20 June 2007).

15   Dickson, *The Elder and His Work*, p. 59.

16   C. H. Spurgeon, Susannah Spurgeon and W. J. Harrald, *C. H. Spurgeon's Autobiography*, vol. i (Pasadena, TX: Pilgrim Publications, 1992), p. 371.

17   Ibid., p. 372.

18   Ibid., p. 371.

19   A helpful resource for thinking further on this issue is Don Whitney's 'Ten Questions to Ask to Turn a Conversation Toward the Gospel' (http://biblicalspirituality.org/gospelq.html (accessed 23 August 2007)).

ABOUT DAY ONE:

Day One's threefold commitment:
- To be faithful to the Bible, God's inerrant, infallible Word;
- To be relevant to our modern generation;
- To be excellent in our publication standards.

I continue to be thankful for the publications of Day One. They are biblical; they have sound theology; and they are relevant to the issues at hand. The material is condensed and manageable while, at the same time, being complete—a challenging balance to find. We are happy in our ministry to make use of these excellent publications.

JOHN MACARTHUR, PASTOR-TEACHER, GRACE COMMUNITY CHURCH, CALIFORNIA

It is a great encouragement to see Day One making such excellent progress. Their publications are always biblical, accessible and attractively produced, with no compromise on quality. Long may their progress continue and increase!

JOHN BLANCHARD, AUTHOR, EVANGELIST AND APOLOGIST

Visit our web site for more information and
to request a free catalogue of our books.

www.dayone.co.uk

Also available

Look after your voice
Taking care of the preacher's
greatest asset

MIKE MELLOR

96PP, PAPERBACK

ISBN 978-1-84625-125-2

As a hammer is to a carpenter, a
scalpel to a surgeon, a trowel to a brick
mason or a needle to a tailor—so the
voice is to a preacher. Man's voice is
the primary means God uses to deliver
His Word to mankind, yet how often
we who are called to impart the most
important truths in the world are apt
to neglect, if not wilfully abuse our
all-vital 'tool of the trade'. Can there
be any more pitiful sight in all nature
than a God-sent preacher who is forced
to be silent? We are not thinking here
however of a silence brought about by
pressure from ungodly sources, but that
which has been enforced because of the
preacher's own negligence concerning
his voice. Mike Mellor's goal is not
to produce another speech book (of
which a good number can be found,
usually aimed at actors or singers) but
that something of our high calling as
God's spokesmen may be re-kindled
and as a consequence our desire to care
for the frail vehicle God has designed
to convey his Word may be increased.

'… I haven't seen anything like it for years,
so it fits a good and helpful niche in the
market … If, like me, you are prepared to
pay the social cost of conditioning your voice
by compulsive 'humming', you should still
buy this little volume for the serious advice it
contains.'

**JONATHAN STEPHEN, PRINCIPAL, WALES
EVANGELICAL SCHOOL OF THEOLOGY AND
DIRECTOR, AFFINITY**

'In much of our modern preaching, a great
deal of catching up is necessary in terms
of actual effective delivery. This book by an
open-air preacher will help us in our public
speaking—even if our voices never have
quite the resonance of a John Chrysostom,
a Whitefield or a Billy Graham. I certainly
intend to put into prayerful practice the
invaluable suggestions and exercises given
us by Mike Mellor.'

**RICO TICE, CO-AUTHOR OF *CHRISTIANITY
EXPLORED* AND ASSOCIATE MINISTER AT
ALL SOULS CHURCH, LONDON**

Also available

Discipline with care
Applying biblical correction in your church

STEPHEN MCQUOID

96PP, PAPERBACK

ISBN 978-1-84625-152-8

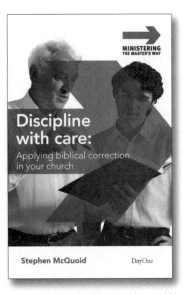

Discipline is one of the most difficult issues in contemporary church life. Church leaders often need to battle to maintain the integrity of their churches, sometimes with tragic results. But why is it so hard? Should we bother with it at all?

In this thorough treatment of the subject, Stephen McQuoid answers these questions and provides a biblical framework for church discipline. Because prevention is better than cure, he shows that discipline is not just about punishing but includes a whole way of life which keeps us spiritually accountable and in a right relationship with God. Corrective discipline will also at times be necessary, and he guides us through the disciplinary stages taught in the New Testament. By using appropriate case studies, he also demonstrates the complications of real-life situations and highlights the lessons that can be learned.

'Stephen McQuoid emphasizes the need for leaders not to shirk the correction of members no matter how difficult. In exercising discipline the church is giving God's verdict on the given situation. There must, therefore, be both judgement and compassion. Helpful advice is given to both leaders and members as to what kind of attitude should be displayed towards the offender.'

DAVID CLARKSON, ELDER AT CARTSBRIDGE EVANGELICAL CHURCH AND AUTHOR OF 'LEARNING TO LEAD' COURSE

'In any local church, the issues of authority, discipline and leadership lie close to the surface. Stephen's book explores succinctly some of the cultural issues, scriptural context and practical outworkings of the vital need to keep the body in shape.'

ANDREW LACEY, CHURCH ELDER, MANAGER GLO BOOK SHOP, DIRECTOR OF PARTNERSHIP, SCOTLAND

Also available

Make your church's money work
Achieving financial integrity in your congregation

JOHN TEMPLE

96PP, PAPERBACK

ISBN 978-1-84625-150-4

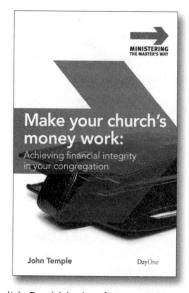

The church's finances are a real concrete expression of its vision, its priorities and its commitment to doing things 'decently and in order'. This book examines the basis of sound biblical stewardship as applied to the practical aspects of budgeting, reporting and control of expenses in a church. It suggests a remuneration policy for pastors and other paid workers and outlines the responsibilities of members in supporting their church. Examples of a spreadsheet for budgeting and reporting are included. It is written in non-accounting terminology and should be read by all leaders and anyone who spends any of the church's money.

'John Temple's book—often provocative, sometimes controversial—uses biblical principles, personal examples and a healthy dose of common sense, as well as giving many practical examples of how church finances could be managed. Few treasurers and leadership teams will fail to benefit from a careful consideration of the principles set out here.'

GARY BENFOLD, PASTOR, MOORDOWN BAPTIST CHURCH, BOURNEMOUTH, ENGLAND

'Make Your Church's Money Work is comprehensive but concise, and easy to read, understand and execute by clergy and laity alike. Its biblical foundation ensures its value and the personal illustrations demonstrate its practicality as a blueprint for fidelity to God and his gospel.'

DR REGGIE WEEMS, SENIOR PASTOR, HERITAGE BAPTIST CHURCH, JOHNSON CITY, TENNESSEE, USA